Núria & Empar Jim
Rosa M. Curto

Taking care of your planet

Yuck!
waste

BARRON'S

Did you know that the garbage generated
by your household during a whole year would
fill up a truck? Just imagine how much waste
a city produces!

Can you imagine what would happen if it were
not collected? It would accumulate in the streets
in really high piles and rats would run around
everywhere. Yuck! It would be really dirty,
wouldn't it? What a smell! And the
problems it would cause!

To live, people need many different things: food, clothing, tools, utensils, furniture, and machines that simplify our lives and make them more comfortable. But all these things we need come from somewhere, and what's more, they produce a lot of waste: food waste, such as peelings, seeds, bottles, boxes, and cans; clothes that are too small for us; old and broken furniture; electrical appliances that are broken or don't work properly; and even medicines that have expired or that we no longer need.

As you can see, it is very easy to create waste at home every day, but it is not so easy to get rid of it.
For this reason, it is very important to reduce the waste.

We can do this in several ways. To start with, we don't need to buy so many unnecessary things. A doll you saw in a store window that you liked a lot, or a ball just like the one your friend Marcos has—buying on a whim doesn't help to reduce waste!

At home, look around your room and in your closet. That red jogging suit, those blue trousers and green shirt that are too small—all those clothes can still be used or reused. There are organizations and secondhand stores that buy and sell everything we no longer need that might be useful to somebody else: clothes and shoes we can no longer wear, books we have read, electrical appliances and furniture we no longer use... Fairs and clothing drives are also held where clothing can be sold or exchanged for other things, or just given away to those in need.

Because your parents know that it is very important not to create so much garbage, they recycle bottles and other containers. Empty bottles and jars can be returned to the store or, if your community provides this service, placed in curbside containers. Glass, plastic, aluminum and other metals are taken to recycling plants, where they are sorted out, cleaned, crushed, and made into new bottles or jars or other products—even road surfaces! Many of these items can be recycled over and over again, so it reduces waste.

Some household waste is so contaminating that it cannot be thrown into any kind of garbage can and it must be taken to a recycling station, where the best way to get rid of it is sought. Some items can be reused, while others may have some parts that can be reused and other parts that must be destroyed to prevent them from polluting the environment.

Did you know that just one tiny broken mercury battery can pollute all the water held in the community swimming pool? Mercury is highly toxic and can kill aquatic animals that come into contact with it.

If you were a magician, you could make this waste disappear with a wave of your magic wand. Whoosh! But because it cannot be made to disappear so easily, it has to be burned or buried underground or treated in special places. This is the best solution that has been found for getting rid of this waste, although it never disappears completely.

Waste is not only generated at home. It is also created when things are produced in farms, mines, and factories—and also when they are transported! Even when we eliminate waste, we create new waste! The residues that leave factories are often dangerous for the environment.

Sometimes, you might find packaging, plastic bags, bottles, and other garbage that people throw on the ground in the parks where you play. It's a shame to go to the mountains and find the place so dirty! Did you know that a simple piece of glass in the forest can cause a fire? You have to be very careful!

And what about the beach and the rivers? All the waste that we throw away can reach the water and damage the animals that live there. Fish, for example, can eat bags and pieces of plastic, metal pop-tops, and cigarette butts, thinking that they are food, like worms or little fish. When they eat so much garbage, they can get sick and die.

Vantu lives on Rapa-Nui, a very small island in the Pacific Ocean. Like many islands in the world, Rapa-Nui generates a lot of waste. The amount of waste is growing increasingly, and there isn't enough space on the island or recycling plants to reuse it or get rid of it. From time to time, special ships have to go there to take away all the waste to the mainland. Transporting waste from one place to another is not the best solution, but if they didn't do this, the small islands would become gigantic garbage dumps.

Waste does not accumulate only on the land and in the sea. Outer space is also full of garbage! Remains of rockets and old satellites rotate around Earth, together with the waste generated by space stations and that left behind by astronauts.

Every day, there is more waste in space because nobody is responsible for collecting it and getting rid of it. Spaceships have a problem: They have to travel very carefully to avoid bumping into the waste!

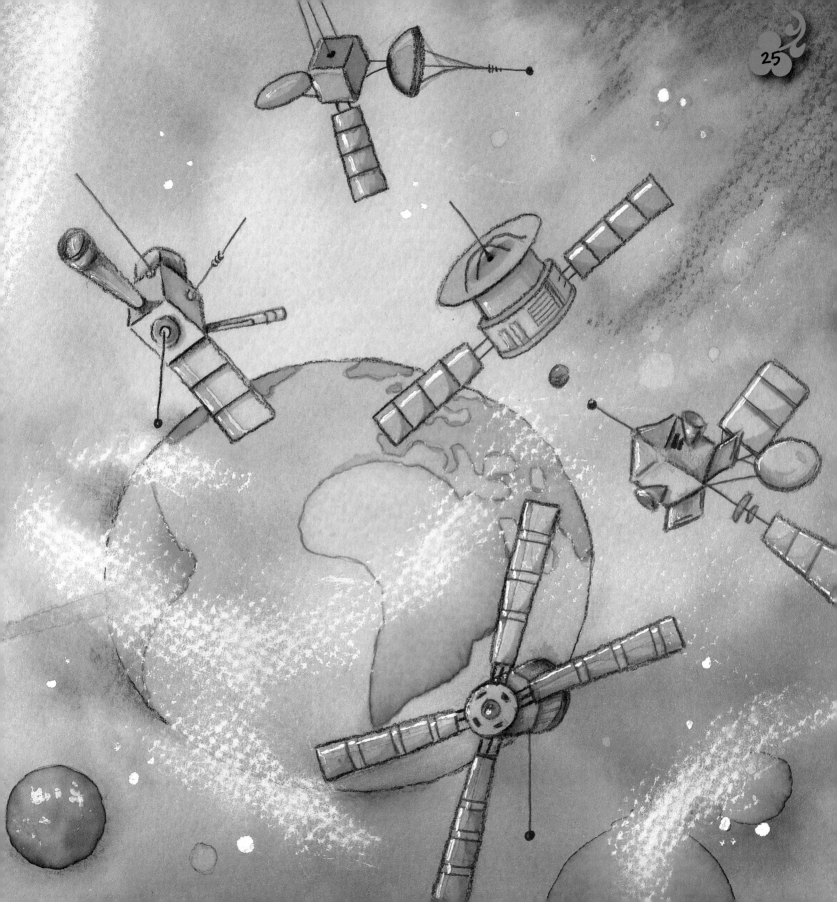

Nature has perfect cycles. Some organisms are producers, others are consumers, and others are decomposers. Thus, the elements necessary for life are recycled and reused, and there is no waste.

Humans change the environment by disrupting the natural cycles. Every time a new product is made and used, artificial materials are created that are not present in nature. The residues of these materials are a serious problem because the organisms present in nature cannot get rid of them in natural cycles.

People should also reduce, reuse, and recycle everything they can, in order to generate as little waste as possible, because, as you have seen, it is very difficult to make waste disappear. We must try not to create any more waste. If we all do our part, we can help clean up our world. I already do my part. You can help, too!

Activities

Cut the plastic

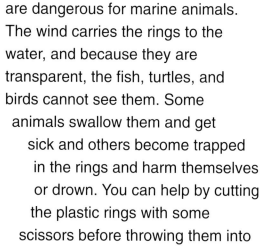

The plastic rings used to join drink cans and bottles together are dangerous for marine animals. The wind carries the rings to the water, and because they are transparent, the fish, turtles, and birds cannot see them. Some animals swallow them and get sick and others become trapped in the rings and harm themselves or drown. You can help by cutting the plastic rings with some scissors before throwing them into the garbage. It's that easy!

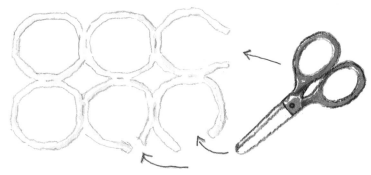

Industrial waste (pages 16–17)

Residues that are not generated in the home generally originate from industry. Ask the children to think about the waste generated by factories: residues from the paper and electronics industries, residue from oil refineries, chemical wastes, medical residues, and so on.

Because it isn't easy to estimate the large quantity of waste produced by the factories of a town over a determined period of time, the previous resource will need some adapting. With a little imagination, the children should see each home in their neighborhood as a kind of industry or service that generates determined residues.

The dangers of waste (pages 18–21)

A walk in the park or a day trip can be used as an excuse to speak about the dangers associated with waste that does not go to a specific place. They will find paper, plastic bags, cigarette butts, pieces of glass, cans, and more.

You can get the children to associate the items they find with potential problems that they can cause. The relation is not always simple or direct. If the children are little, help them to understand the dangers: water and soil pollution, landscape degradation, fire risks, and so on.

In the mountains or forest, they will find waste that is not recent and can take many years to disintegrate. This can help you introduce the concept of average lifespan.

Vantu's island (pages 22–23)

The island of Rapa-Nui, also called Easter Island, is an example of the problems associated with waste. Until recently, its inhabitants lived from fishing and raising livestock and they didn't have many material needs.

The arrival of manufactured products to the island has contributed to improving the quality of life. However, it has caused the inhabitants to generate a large quantity of residues that they cannot manage on the island and that have to be exported to the continent. Awareness of the need to reduce waste has increased, because Chile has restricted bringing waste into the country.

On another scale, planet Earth is also an island. It might appear that we have the capacity to absorb the waste we generate, but what will happen if we continue to produce waste at the current rate? Will the rich countries pay the poorest ones to take care of it?

The organic cycle (pages 26–27)

In nature, the waste produced by some organisms is the food source of others. You can work on this topic using building blocks to create different "organisms." When one dies (it can be dismantled), other organisms can grow or be born. You can explain the organic cycles to older children. In the carbon cycle, for example, plants incorporate carbon dioxide to "produce" new biomass. The plants are eaten by animals and fungi and the microorganisms decompose them to generate carbon dioxide once again.

In principle, all natural organic substances can end up being "recycled." Recently, artificial materials have been created that end up in the environment. The problem is that they are very persistent and no microorganisms exist that are able to break them down. These substances can have very harmful effects on the environment and human health.

Yuck! waste

Original title of the book in Catalan:
Cuidem el Planeta: Ecs! Els Residus
© Copyright Gemser Publications S.L., 2010.
C/ Castell, 38; Teià (08329) Barcelona, Spain (World Rights)
Tel: 93 540 13 53
E-mail: info@mercedesros.com
Website: www.mercedesros.com
Authors: Núria & Empar Jiménez
Illustrator: Rosa María Curto

First edition for the United States and Canada published
2010 by Barron's Educational Series, Inc.

All inquiries should be addressed to:
Barron's Educational Series, Inc.
250 Wireless Boulevard
Hauppauge, New York 11788
www.barronseduc.com

ISBN-13: 978-0-7641-4546-9
ISBN-10: 0-7641-4546-0

Library of Congress Control No.: 2009943887

Manufactured by: L. Rex Printing Co. LTD.,
Tin Wan, China
Date of Manufacture: August 2010

Printed in China
9 8 7 6 5 4 3 2 1